THE SOLOMON PAPERS

MURRY GRANT GUDMUNDSON

TREATY OAK PUBLISHERS

PUBLISHER'S NOTES

Copyright © 2025 by Murry Grant Gudmundson
All rights reserved.

This book or any portion thereof may not be reproduced, distributed, or transmitted in any form or by any means without the express written consent of the copyright holder, except in the case of brief quotations for the purpose of reviews and certain other noncommercial uses permitted by copyright law.

Front cover art by Madison Land
Back cover art by Lisa Baptiste
Cover design by Kimberly Greyer

Printed and published in the United States of America

ISBN-978-1-959127-41-3

Available in print and digital from Amazon

Treaty Oak Publishers
www.treatyoakpublishers.com

DEDICATION

to my wife, Valerie

TABLE OF CONTENTS

Foreword - 1-4

Tuesday Meditation Class - 5-6

Eternal Light - 7-10

The "As If" Principle - 11-12

Ego - Friend and Enemy - 13-14

Ego and Consciousness - 15-18

Energy - Motion - 19-20

Forgiveness and Healing - 21-24

The Gift - Heart - 25-26

Mortality and Beyond - 27-30

Release - Letting Go - 31-32

Sustain - 33-34

The Solomon Papers Class - OFFER - 35-36

Life Saver - 37-38

Acknowledgments - 39

About the Author - 41-42

FOREWORD

I was born in Salt Lake City, Utah, in 1939 and raised in the L.D.S. (Mormon) tradition. My childhood could be described as normal in every way. My parents were loving and supportive of me and my older brother, Tom. A feeling of love was always in our home. Of course, there were the occasional issues and challenges that all families experienced from time to time.

"Spiritual" experiences were common in my family, and I was encouraged to accept them as special and sacred. I was also counseled to avoid the popular games of the day, such as the Ouija board and other similar games, which my parents believed were "of the devil," a concept I accepted until my early adulthood.

When I was five years old, my family moved to southern California, and there continued a good and stable environment. By the time I reached the age of about eight or nine, I had experienced a series of very unusual dreams that were quite spiritual in nature. To this day, I hold them as very special and personal.

One experience I can share is a series of several dreams in which I was in direct and personal contact with the creator. In fact, we played and conversed as if we were very best friends. The only problem was his regular and often sudden disappearance without warning, and I was left alone until the next dream.

It was very frustrating, but I eventually accepted it when a silent voice told me the disappearances were necessary and I would understand in time. As the months passed, those dreams became a thing of the past and were replaced by much greater dreams. The series of dreams triggered many personal lessons and are still an important part of my life to this day.

One of those lessons was to accept and enjoy my relationship with the Divine. I take those experiences and apply them in my everyday life. I learned that the creator did not abandon me as I assumed. He simply became invisible but never left. As time passed, I learned I could go within and find the guidance I needed. I didn't always have to depend on dreams for that connection. Of course, even today, the occasional dream comes, and I still cherish every memory of those experiences.

In retrospect, I believe those dreams and other personal experiences were the beginnings of what later became the foundation of my participation in the world of Metaphysics.

In the mid-1970s, while taking a psychology class (Psychology 101), I accepted an assignment to write a paper on E.S.P. For background information, I attended a series of group meetings with others who had personal experiences with psychic awareness. There, I met two men who became my mentors and best friends for several years. Between the group meetings and casual sharing of personal experiences with those and other friends, my paper was the catalyst that changed my life.

Just a few years after writing that paper, I had the privilege of attending an intensive class on the practical and spiritual application of metaphysics. It was then that I had a formal introduction to my personal spirit guides and teachers.

Just for the record, I do believe in angels, spirit guides, and teachers, including other enlightened beings in spirit. I was also ready to be convinced that those special beings could be a part of the highest regions of my own superconscious. It appears to me those regions are equal to those angels and teachers in the spirit realm. In other words, enlightened beings of spirit are identical to the highest aspects of the "superconscious" part of the mind. Regardless of one's belief system, *The Solomon Papers* can offer great comfort and direction to any open-minded reader, whether it be from that high aspect of my super-consciousness or spirit guides such as The Solomon.

I had been aware of spirit guides and guardian angels for quite some time before I attended that intensive metaphysical class in Salt Lake City. After the two-week series ended, as I was driving home I had an overwhelming urge to pull off to the side of the road and wait. I knew something very profound was about to happen but didn't quite know what.

After a moment or two, a very powerful and gentle silent voice said, "Our beloved, we have been part of you since before the beginning. We have always been a part of you, and you have been a part of us forever. Because of your thirst for knowledge and, more importantly, wisdom, you may call us 'Solomon'. We are not the Solomon of the Old Testament. However, we could be perceived more as of the 'soul of man'.

"Remember! As you travel through your life, always endeavor to function with integrity, bringing with you compassion, perseverance, and continual forgiveness, beginning with yourself. We are always with you! When you seek our counsel, quiet your mind and simply ask, and we will respond. Be sure to be in tune with the principles we mentioned, and as you listen, you will hear."

Just to be clear, I refer to my guides and teachers in Spirit as "The Solomon" because, as I understand it, they are a group of twelve. I've been told I am a part of that twelve. "Spirit" communicates with individuals in a way they can understand and accept, a phrase I use often. "The words of a lesson are very important. However, the learning, understanding, and applying of that lesson is the most important of all."

The Solomon Papers are a collection of personal conversations I have had over the years. It is my understanding that those teachers in spirit use my mind and certain aspects of my body to communicate. In other words, The Solomon communicates in thought patterns and can present an infinite amount of information in a micro-mini-second. My body and mind organize that information in a linear way that one can understand and accept.

The Solomon Papers are just a small part of what I have received over the years, but if they are received and interpreted with a pure and honest heart, they will provide a significant amount of encouragement and hope.

Anyone can receive inspiration and information from guides, teachers, and angels. It is NOT exclusive to me or anyone else. Always consider the contents of this work and others. Think about it. Meditate on it. Use what you feel is right for you. Live it with honesty and compassion for yourself and those who cross your path.

As you read this work, please read it with an open mind, think about what you receive, meditate, and pray about it. If it resonates in a positive way for you, then and only then, incorporate it into your life and take responsibility for what you do with it!

TUESDAY MEDITATION CLASS

For several years, I've been teaching meditation classes on Tuesday evenings. This has been a great source of information and growth for me and for those who have attended, particularly those who regularly perform the homework assignments.

In the last few years, the homework assignments have often been a single word or simple phrase that the students contemplate and ask their guides and angels to suggest ways to apply what they were given. This has been extremely fruitful and enlightening as we build upon our awareness.

In this book, I offer channelings from The Solomon, which I received when doing the assigned homework.

ETERNAL LIGHT

As I have been contemplating the nature of Light, several things have come to mind, many of which have already been discussed in my meditation class and private readings. I'm hoping these perspectives will help me understand more about how it affects us personally. I am profoundly grateful to The Solomon for stimulating my thought process to the point that I've been able to put into words a few of the concepts that mean so much to me and, I hope, to those who may take the time to read and contemplate these words, too.

Good morning, Solomon! Would you please help me understand the concept of Light and how it relates to healing?

Beloved!
It is the primary reflection of Light that heals in the physical world.
Allow us to share with you some of the attributes of this principle: To eternal Light, there has never been a beginning, and there will never be an end. It has no polarity, and because of this, it is infinite.
Light's primary reflection heals.
Four additional terms, like Light, are also without a beginning or end. These are Love, Spirit, Truth, and Consciousness. We will discuss these at another time. As Light, none of these terms is subject to time and space, but their applications are finite because they do have polarity with a beginning and an eventual end.

Whatever the application, there are fragments of those principles in all the others. Therefore, they are always present to some degree in all applications on any "level." *They are the very essence of the eternal "now."*

The Greater Light in its purity can only be perceived by reflection. We will always refer to this reflection in lower-case because it is energy, therefore physical and mortal. The light you perceive with your physical eyes and other senses comprises photons and other elements. It is, therefore, part of the physical realm and, as such, will ultimately cease to exist. It is that reflection most often referred to as light; it is light energy generated by the sun and all other stars in the universe. The light of day, the lights you see from the fixtures in your homes and outdoors, only reveal reflections of the Greater Light.

When one sends a kind thought to another, it is the best reflection of light sent and received. Since Light is ever present and within all things. Even reflections that are not so positive or loving have the presence of The Greater Light somewhere within them. *All things in the universe exist with the presence of that Greater Light.*

Light created the material universe, and the sun maintains it. The sun is our only source of that reflector. The countless stars are suns, and they are necessary to contain and prolong the life source of the universe. Should all the stars in the heavens cease to exist, being would still exist, but it would not express itself in anything physical.

Surrounding or simply sending light to a person, place, or circumstance is good and positive. It is effective and helps to support the expression of light throughout the entire planet and beyond. Everything, positive or negative, reflects light, or it could not exist.

Often, certain colors found in light energy are used to increase and specialize the healing energies. However, crystal clear light is often the most effective and can be used anytime and anywhere. The intent of the sender is by far the most important element in offering healing energy. One color is not better or worse than another. When working with light, it is always appropriate to use pure, crystal-clear light. *Remember, light and its primary reflection are always pure.*

It is also important to realize that in the material universe, the colors the naked eye sees are actually distortions, but they have very specific benefits for the physical realm.

As you send light and kind healing thoughts to someone, you activate an automatic process that infuses your entire being with portions of the light that the recipient's aura, when ready, will also receive. Since Light is infinite, it is capable of staying in an individual with its bonded thought forms until the time is right for it to enter. When the person is ready, he or she will receive the fullness of the healing light energy that awaits. That healing energy remains with the recipient until it enters and completes its intended purpose. *Again, healing comes only through light.*

All healing procedures allow the body to receive a specific reflection of the Greater Light, and a degree of wholeness can be restored. Again, there is no discord or dis-ease in the purity of Light and its primary reflection, light.

As an exercise, we urge you to imagine yourself as if you are pure, crystal-clear light in your present human form. This process helps to educate your body and mind to be more clearly attuned and more "enlightened" to the light you seek and ready for the light as it is offered to you.

Be of the light!

Be in the light!

Be light itself.

Please be always mindful that you are, for now, a carrier of light, and one day, when you are in the space between the spaces, you will become that very light.

Again, Light is infinite and does not depend on motion to exist. The energy that reflects it will exist for as long as there is motion. It is light that heals. Intentions, thoughts, prayers, and other enlightened thought energies will carry that light to the receiver and create great benefits for the sender as well.

Always remember that mankind has made great progress in creating certain tools that can help the body heal. It is appropriate to use those tools when needed. But also always remember that these tools help to clear the path for the light to accomplish the actual healing. Be wise; be ready to use any and all available tools and actions to heal the body and the mind. *The soul and spirit depend exclusively on Light to be made whole.*

Continue to attune yourself to the Light, follow its pure reflection, and follow your chosen path in life. We will continue the journey with you.

Thank you, Solomon!

More to come

THE "AS IF" PRINCIPLE

Good morning, Solomon!

In my meditation class, we have discussed the process of consciously creating our "reality." I have introduced a concept I learned years ago called the 'As If Principle'. Would you please elaborate on this so I can understand and share it more clearly?

Good morning to you, Beloved!
The "As If" principle is one of the simpler yet complicated concepts to understand. Applying a measure of wisdom can be an extremely valuable and useful tool for becoming the 'conscious creator' you are created to be.

When a thought is placed into motion, it is already creating its fulfillment somewhere in the universe. Thinking as if it is already coming about in your personal realm of experience makes the probabilities of that fulfillment and closure far more likely. This principle also requires a clear presence of personal faith. Without that faith, the "As If" principle does not function as well.

This principle can be used in a positive or a negative way. For example, one using wisdom will soon realize that thinking "as if" a certain painful or tragic experience never happened, or perhaps trying to create something simply out of harmony with the Truth, is clearly using similar energy. This principle has an entirely different application and does not apply here. In other words, one can create anything based on Light or the "shadows" where free will determines which polarity it will be.

The "As If" principle works best when it is applied by thinking "as if" the result can be completely dealt with and "as if" the final effect is becoming a conscious energy for the greatest good. This principle also puts one's thinking clearly in the present and assumes the thought is already there and functioning perfectly.

Using the "As If" principle with additional compatible thoughts and actions will add energy and legitimacy to what's being created. When the process is finished, the thought will have been created in a perfect way. It is said that as one thinks in and from the heart, that thought has no choice but to appear in some form in the universe. It will either contribute to its creator's best good or demise. *When becoming a conscious creator, one must be using wisdom, or this principle can be far less than enlightened.*

Everything about the "As If" principle goes far deeper than it may appear on the surface. This precept is at the very core of creativity and is always in play, whether or not one is consciously aware of it.

It is wise to treat this principle with great reverence and respect. It can and will bring about perfect reflections of your innermost perceptions of and what you perceive about yourself and your place in the universe.

EGO – FRIEND AND ENEMY

Hello, Solomon! Many people, including myself, have had serious conflicts with the ego. Would you please share some perspective on this subject so I can understand it better and share it with others who are seeking to comprehend it?

Beloved,
Much has been written on this subject, and it seems, for most, to be just a little out of reach for a truly satisfying definition. The clearest for you to understand is that the ego is your mind on all levels.

Would you care to explain further?

There seems to be a battle between the heart and the ego. That which comes purely through the heart is light and truth. That which comes from the ego could have a glimmer of truth but will never be complete.
The sole purpose of the ego is survival. Whatever it takes to further that perception, the ego is fully on board.

It can inspire.

It can devastate and bring about an infinite number of emotions in between.
Again, whatever it takes to guarantee survival, the ego will do. It will lead you toward the Light but will never get you there.
There will always be just one more class, one more seminar, or one more book to read. It will show fragments of truth but never the fullness of it.
The ego (mind) is constantly in motion because it has polarity.

Therefore, it cannot be completely truthful.

Truth never moves because it is without polarity.

Because the ego is forever in motion, it can only reveal reflections of truth at best.

EGO AND CONSCIOUSNESS

Message from The Solomon

"Continue to reconcile ego with consciousness."

Consciousness is the principle on which the entire physical universe depends for its existence. To be even clearer, consciousness is the principle in which all physical forms exist. Your universe is only one of an infinite number of similar creations.

The Ego is the mind—conscious, subconscious, superconscious—or any other form that exists in the physical realm. The Ego maintains your existence in the universe, and it exists to keep you there at all costs. This is the reason for the seeming conflict that Ego has with consciousness as you know it. Were this conflict to cease to exist, there would be no need to experience your place in this universe.

Some say that the ego must die. This may be correct at some point in the far distant future when all things in the material universe have been fulfilled. The truth is, at this time, the Ego must not die but ultimately be reconciled with consciousness. When this occurs, one can eventually experience all that is—simultaneously. When one becomes consciously aware, concepts and fragments of a greater "reality" come to mind, and another step in that reconciliation is created. *This is one of the great advantages of meditation.*

Whether active or passive, meditation infuses light into the Ego (mind) and enables one the opportunity to be more consciously aware. Thus, one takes another step toward that ultimate reconciliation of the finite with the infinite. One's own personal progress is not hard to see as one becomes more and more consciously mindful of the way one thinks today compared with one's thought processes of the past.

In years past, much was said about the end of 2012. Many feared the earth would end and humanity would be no more. This was a blatant misunderstanding that caused far too much unnecessary stress and anxiety among many. It also triggered some to avoid taking that predicted time seriously. It acted as a catalyst. Both ways of thinking are ego-orientated and do not support the loving nature of existence.

If you consider these past few years seriously, you will see that your world has endured profound changes. Many of these came with a great deal of chaos, pain, destruction, and confusion. We say to you this will indeed continue for some time to come. It will last until a clear awakening and profound shift in humanity's awareness occurs.

With some meditative thought, you will see that these difficult changes result from the unbridled ego and its destructive energies, which will continue for some time to come.

The law of polarity assures that the opposite is also true. Many have already embarked on a path of greater enlightenment and a clearer sense of love and many of its applications. If you were to perceive the incredible scope of the love that created your existence, you would soon be filled with the confidence, compassion, and vision to truly contribute to the healing that must eventually come. Use this concept as one of the elements at the foundation of your awareness and, one day, experience the vast scope of the healing to which you have contributed.

The present is an extremely important time. It would be advantageous to approach your future with a sense of reverence, confidence, and hope. This will be a time when a window will open and literally pour out a great infusion of potential. Many will feel the profound transformation that will first occur within and then manifest itself in daily life.

In the end, humankind will have the opportunity to either transform into a greater reality, in which this planet will enter, or start the cycle all over again. *Either way, the light will prevail.*

The more you engage in meditation and act upon the conscious awareness that follows each experience, the more likely you will be aware of your own transformation and that of the others you influence, which are many.

Please understand that if one chooses not to pass through the portal of transformation, this does NOT mean they need to start from the beginning. They will simply choose to begin their growth cycle from where they are now. Eventually, when the earth transforms, there will be other worlds for those who choose it to live on and continue their experiences. They will choose this by using their own free will. You will also notice some who simply do not seem capable of comprehending the laws and principles of intention and the finer points of the Metaphysical points of view.

Many of these people have already experienced what they need and are here merely to live those principles and are no doubt more ready for transition than you may think. It is not given to you to know about the progress of every person that comes into your life. *All people are students and teachers at the same time.*

For those who do choose to step through the portal of 2012, some will experience almost an immediate change of perception. New people and circumstances will manifest in individual lives, and the growth will be almost spectacular. However, for the most part, the transition will be far more subtle.

A slightly expanded understanding of the laws of the universe will manifest, and then, more and more will be given.

The rate of growth and change will be much clearer and faster. For most people, the transformation has already begun and will receive a significant push as the year approaches its final days.

There are countless realms of existence. The physical universe is only one. We, Solomon, exist in a realm that is compatible with the earth plane. What you perceive as the world of spirit is also a compatible realm as well as many others that do not concern you at this time. As you pass through the portal of 2012, a finer harmonic will become more apparent, and communications between the spirit world and ours will become clearer and much more healing.

As you meditate regularly, you are training yourself and others to manage this transition more comfortably and quickly. You will still have contact with those who have not chosen the transition if you wish. With some, it will be an act of compassion as much as any other motivation. Many relationships will be completed, and others that are more compatible with the transition will take place. In a manner of speaking, this is already taking place, but on a much simpler scale.

As you contemplate these words, more understanding will come. Your vision of the concept of spirit will develop at a faster rate. *Be careful always to be compassionate and patient with those who are struggling.* All those who awaken to the light accept responsibility for that awakening. Part of that responsibility is to help those in need, whatever that need may be. Be sure to attune yourself to the light as much as possible. In doing this, you will be given the knowledge on exactly how to be of help. Sometimes, that knowledge will guide you to lovingly leave things alone and let spirit do its job.

We are confident that speaking in ways you can understand and accept will allow you to reap much more than might be on the printed page. Be patient, contemplate these things often, and we will whisper peace to your soul and encourage continued service as long as you are willing. *Always keep an awareness of the light that you are, and you will be guided in every aspect of your being.*

You have been guided to speak of some of the principles of alchemy in your classes. Many will perceive beyond the words and come to a quiet understanding of how this ancient art fits so well with the transformations to come. Transformation is the precursor to transmuting body, soul, and spirit.

ENERGY – MOTION

Hello, Solomon! Would you please share with me a few concepts about light and energy?

Beloved, thank you for having the attunement to ask!

There has never been a beginning or end to Light. The Law of Polarity is the first manifestation of Light in the physical universe. Without it, energy could not exist, and nothing could ever be created. To say, "Let there be Light," means to "put into motion" or "bring into being." All being is in motion. When you become aware of a need, it is most effective to say with a sense of faith and confidence, "Let …"

It is true that the creative force of the universe has no concept of time and space. Everything is one: one in purpose, one in being, one in love, the almighty ONE. To bring the "all-mighty One" into an elemental realm, such as the frequency of matter, requires a partnership with a higher power, the Creator. Through this partnership, the creative energies are attracted to the combined acceptance of the receiver and the will of the Creator.

Remember, the creative forces do not have senses as you know them, although all the elements of the senses are within them. Therefore, you, the receiver, must put that creative energy into the physical world and see that it makes sense.

You are a creator in the act of becoming. Were you not becoming, you would not be in motion. If you were not in motion, you would not have the need for any lessons, feelings, joys, or sorrows.

You would have no needs.

You would be part of the realm of the "no-thing."

Enjoy your "being-ness." Feel free to create! You are limited only by your imagination and willingness to accept. Remember, this existence on the earth illusion is to practice, to grow, to experience, and to accept the mantle of Creator. We salute you! We honor you! We love and support all that you are!

*The "no-thing" is that which exists with no polarity. Some call it "the limitless light."

More to come!

FORGIVENESS AND HEALING

Hello, Solomon!
   Over the years, I have sat in counsel with many clients and friends who are in terrible circumstances or are dealing with an awful disease of body or mind. Many have said with great sincerity and in obvious pain:

"What have I done to deserve this?"

"Am I such a bad person?"

"Who have I offended?"

"Why would a loving God allow me to be in such pain?"

I can relate to these feelings because I've experienced many of the same things these people have shared with me. For years, I have been aware that diseases of the body and outer circumstances reflect disorders in the mind and/or soul. Would you please comment on this and shed some light from your perspective?

Beloved,
We understand these emotions, and we are here to soothe your wounds. We are here to heal. We are here to assist you. We are not here to experience for you or to influence your life's contract in one way or another. You, however, have the tools within you and the free will to change or supplement it. You are a creator, and you have the potential within you to change your life for better or worse.
   It is a matter of simply changing and expanding your thought arena

ever so slightly.

We are here for you.

All you need to do is allow us to come to you through your heart center. This is the only way for us to assist you.

Touch the crystal in your heart. Truly feel it. Though symbolic, it is not the crystal that shields you from your fears and all other issues that may interrupt your sense of peace.

Be not afraid!

Allow yourself to forgive.

This is the foundation of all pain. Forgiveness of self and all others on all levels of existence is the key to changing the circumstances of your life, whatever they may be.

Make no mistake. Forgiveness seems like a simple thing, but we promise you it is a very profound principle and is the gateway to peace in body, soul, and spirit. Learn, understand, and implement this principle in every respect.

The principle of forgiveness releases unnecessary defenses that block the flow of pure light. *The flow of light is the foundation of healing.*

Forgiveness is also a process because it is connected with the physical. As you begin to truly forgive, your thought process automatically expands, and you put yourself in an enlightened environment that allows angels and other beings of light to make themselves known to you. With this expanded way of thinking, you naturally remove your ego from the "dis-ease" you are experiencing. First, the emotional pain and anxieties will disappear, and then the physical healing has a chance to take place. *Be patient, this process could take a fair amount of time!*

The speed at which this process occurs depends entirely on how completely your expanded thinking takes place, and the principle of forgiveness becomes a permanent part of your reality. You will likely slide in and out of this dimension of thought until you truly can maintain it on all levels.

Again, be patient with yourself. This process takes time. As you accomplish this state of being, you will discover more and more expanded perceptions are available to you. They have been a part of you all along. You are simply expanding your awareness to perceive them.

One of the reasons you are expressing in a physical body at this time is to rediscover who you are. The knowledge you are seeking is, in fact, very old knowledge and is already a part of you. We support you in your re-discovery! *Claim it! Use it wisely and become it forever.*

Forgiveness is the release of resentment or the claim to reprisal. It also means making allowances for errors or weaknesses. We use this terminology for your convenience and understanding. In many cases, forgiveness is simple and comes without much thought or action. However, in the context we are addressing, it is a profound and life-changing concept not to be taken lightly. Look beyond the words and discover their intent. Then, you will grasp the full healing nature of forgiveness.

Releasing diseases and surrendering bring genuine peace. This peace is the theater in which the healing process flourishes. Whatever the difficulty or level of pain, the healing process is the same, and the principle of forgiveness is the catalyst for its success.

Wisdom allows appropriate procedures and techniques that become available to assist in the healing process and help to relieve many of the symptoms. *But without forgiveness, no healing is complete.*

More to come!

THE GIFT – HEART

This channeling came about quite spontaneously as I was meditating several years ago. I feel that it is just as poignant today as it was at the time it was given.
Get out of your head and into your heart!

We love you and are here for you. You are trying too hard. Follow your own counsel and try easy! Remember to:

LET there be Light.

Let THERE be light.

Let there be LIGHT.

Letting is the key to creativity. Letting is that which allows creativity to flow with ease and purpose. Letting implies a partnership with the creator.
With that partnership, all things are possible.
Even the monumental task of forgiving oneself can be accomplished by simply letting it happen. As always, we are with you! We love you, and we understand your fears, for they are great. We offer you comfort. Keep focused. Let your intent be. It has already come to fruition and will be in you very soon.
Rage does not dissolve rage.
Vengeance will not make despair go away.
Only the Light of Love can break through the darkness and bring the brilliance of the dawn. Learn of Love, take the knowledge to your Heart, and *let its Light radiate in you and through you. It is the only way to peace.*
Until the Light of compassion dissolves the darkness of rage, it sits and

festers until it destroys the very fabric of the soul. Things said in rage and gross anger have little light and will fade quickly in the face of light and forgiveness. Make no mistake; there are consequences for actions. For this is a basic law of this frequency you call the earth. In spirit, the serenity and peace of being is not ever disturbed.

You do not yet have the understanding necessary to put this principle into practice. But you are very close. Keep up your good work. Work on your self-imposed limitations, and we will send an army of angels to support you in your desires and intentions.

We accept the love you have shared with us, and we return it with compassion and a great understanding of your pain. We are with you in joy and in sorrow. *Use your imagination*, and let us comfort and support you,

Make good use of your day.

In love and service,

More to come!

MORTALITY AND BEYOND

This is a communication given during a meditation. It was spontaneous, as many others have been from time to time. I hope you will find this enlightening and useful. I did.

Beloved!

As you have been informed time after time, you are a creator.

You and all other human beings do so with every thought and every beat of the heart. You are now creating the circumstances that will ultimately bring you the fulfillment of your earthly contract (karma). You are also creating the circumstances that will accommodate your reality while in this life and after you leave it as well.

The universe and all that is within it, must reach its ultimate fulfillment and eventually end. This is NOT an end to being because creating is always partly eternal and is not confined to things physical. There has never been a beginning or an end.

Therefore, there will always be a physical dimension, and there will always be those in spirit who will feel the need and volunteer to temporarily inhabit physical bodies and experience forgetting the spirit realm. By doing this, they will be accepting the responsibility that comes with free will. Be aware that there is still a fragment of remembering the world of spirit, which is deeply embedded within the inner mind and can, on occasion, be accessed through meditation and other related means.

When your purpose is fulfilled in this life, you will go on to other dimensions well beyond your present ability to conceive or comprehend. We share this information with you at this time so you will become aware that there is far, far more to Truth and Light than you are capable of perceiving or understanding in your earthly existence alone. The human brain is simply not capable of processing those concepts.

All other worlds in the universe are mortal and exist in energy fields in harmony with that level of existence. The earth is also in this harmonious field and is subject to the same laws of mortality. Some of those worlds are approaching the very edge of the physical universe. It does not matter how close they are to that edge. They are still mortal and are still within the bounds of physical existence.

An interesting thing would be that as those fringes are approached, there will always be more creation that will expand those borders accordingly. Therefore, there will always be energies similar to that of the earth, and there will always be human beings who will inhabit them.

When that experience is fulfilled, you and others like you will go on to other totally different realms. *What a wonderful thing is consciousness!*

You and all other humans are not yet capable of even being aware of the specifics of these states of being. There is no motion there, as you know it. There is no polarity; it is the realm of the no-thing "limitless light."

Finally, you and all human beings truly have no beginning and no end. Your earthly existence is but a flash in the greater realities of The Limitless Light. *Of this, you can be sure!*

The earth's frequency is rapidly coming into attunement with another of the "harmonics" of the Light. This is one of the reasons the grid that surrounds the earth is being re-aligned. When this re-alignment is completed, a new perception of color will be available to those who are willing to see it. The powers of perception will be expanded, the senses will be quickened, and the knowledge of love will go to yet another level.

There is much more to this, most of which will be presented as you and others are more prepared. Contemplate these things and become more aware of their boundless potential. Be warned that ego is a part of this energy, and it must be harnessed and directed in a far more enlightened way. *This is essential!*

Ego will challenge you and others in ways you thought to be impossible. To prepare you for this greater path, *remember that with experience comes knowledge.*

The new path we speak of is a path of knowledge, understanding, and wisdom. Can you see that you must "experience" all things to "know" all things? When this is accomplished, you will be able to travel this new path with ease and purpose. You will see this path to be very exciting, and you will have earned the opportunity to travel it.

We celebrate you for this.

The admonitions you have received in the past few years are essential for you to incorporate into your new experiences. As you do this, your aura will automatically adjust, and you will be attracting entirely new experiences, new people, and new circumstances. Those who are willing to grow in the same direction will be with you still.

Those who do not desire or have not perceived themselves as capable of this new direction will be equally loved and supported but will be successfully pursuing a more compatible path for their awareness and experience.

There is nothing new about this concept. But it may, indeed, bring some clarity to some of the unspoken feelings you've had about the changes you've seen coming in the very near future.

You are still selected to teach and heal in your chosen way. You will soon be seeing more individual clients. Your style of counseling will change dramatically. You will be addressing most of those individuals through a more evolved energy that is being placed between the steps of the latter of your DNA structure and the fluids that support it. This is the entrance to the "space between the spaces."

This is totally in the energy of the DNA at this point. This is part of the preparation for the final Physical changes. In other words, you and a few others are observing and will be able to better function with your angels in the space between the spaces.

Meditate and contemplate this. As you do so, the other references you have received about this concept will fall into place.

Enjoy the ride! It's one that few have even dreamed of.

There is much, much more to come. We are aware that this message is different from many of the others you have received.

The love is real and constant.
The personal regard is also real and constant.

These things are intended to magnify your ability and skill in being of the best service to those who are so greatly loved.

RELEASE - LETTING GO

Good morning, Solomon.

Through the years, I've come to appreciate the value of release. Would you please share with me some information from your perspective that will give me a greater sense of personal direction?.

Beloved!
The goal has been to become fully aware of the Light that I am. When you come to that realization, all those terms will make total sense, and you will have a complete understanding of the difference between eternal light and its primary reflection, which is the light we deal with in the physical universe.
Release is returning to the Light. *For you, our beloved, to understand this process is to understand the nature of Light and its reflections.*

Thank you, please continue.

Light, Love, Consciousness, and Truth are infinite terms because they have no polarity. Therefore, they are eternal and do not move. They are all the same but have distinct applications and impact the physical universe differently. Because they are infinite, their applications are all in harmony with all that is. For this discussion, we will focus on Light and its reflection.
The physical universe and all that is in it depends on the law of polarity, which is the essence of motion (energy). This law is the very foundation of all things physical. Without it, energy could not exist, and there would be no motion, no energy, and no universe. *It is essential for you to understand polarity.* All its reflections are subject to the laws

and principles of this illusion known as the physical realm.

The Light is who and what you are and will be forever! The more you attune yourself to this principle, the more you will understand the concept of releasing yourself from all that is contrary to Light and its infinite reflections. Light is the essence of existence and is the foundation of every living person, place, and thing. The amount and purity of this energy depend on your perceptions and personal values.

Remember, Light itself has no polarity and is yet the very principle that supports the existence of the universe itself. The energy we call light is the reflection of Light and supports the structure of all things physical.

Releasing is reflective energy and its resulting thought forms. It is those thought forms that can discourage you from truly becoming the Light (Love) that you are, have been, and will be forever more. As you relax and trust the process of release, you will continue becoming more aware of the Light that you are. Then, you are more likely to let go and release the things that block that awareness.

Release is a divine thing. By releasing your fears and limited perceptions of yourself, it becomes more automatic, and peace of body and soul soon reveals itself.

As you let go of your illusions, fears, and anxieties blocking your sense of peace, it will surely dissolve. You will see the reflection of that peace becoming brighter and brighter within yourself. As you continue to experience the process of surrender (letting go), what you perceive in the see, touch, hear, smell, and taste world is a perfect reflection of the very foundation of yourself.

Continue to love, respect, and admire the Light you already are. Release those things that block the Light and see your world change. The miracle of you becomes even more radiant and able to bring about the wonderful work you have come here to do. *You are the miracle!* It is the magnificent you that makes the difference in the universe. Clarify and purify your perceptions of self, and you will change the universe.

All are one! All are creators!
More to come!

SUSTAIN

Solomon!

The homework word for the meditation class students to contemplate and inquire about is "Sustain." Would you please share some insight on how to apply this in my personal life?

Beloved!
We are always available, and the quality of your response from us or anyone in Spirit depends on your level of trust and personal attunement.

"Sustain" is one of those words that reflects the results of your perceptions and values, not just for you but for all of those who affect your aura. To sustain is to support and assist in one's withstanding that which distracts or causes a loss of determination to complete an activity or perception.

You are accomplishing a personal commitment to support and sustain the great work of healing the hearts and souls of your fellow beings. Some understand your commitment and will sustain you with their words and deeds of comfort and enthusiasm. Others who believe in the work you are doing will sustain you with money.

We, The Solomon, sustain you by constantly feeding your countenance and the clearer regions of your mind with the energies and thoughts necessary for you to continue with health, power, and confidence,

Of course, the Earth is sustained by all the laws and energies that the Universe has to offer. The Earth is further sustained by the thoughts and loving energies sent by those of us in Spirit who have a sacred interest in the growth and success that was intended from the beginning.

The law of polarity also demands the existence of the opposite as well. Entities and energies are in place whose sole purpose is to decay and ultimately destroy your world before its time. These energies exist in the shadows of darkness in and around the Earth, and they are only too eager to continue and accomplish their purposes.

We urge you to avoid giving any unnecessary energy to these entities and their forces. *Remember, darkness cannot exist in Light*. Always radiate Light around and through your world. This is the most effective way you can help the healing forces at this time.

Much more to come!

Thank you, Solomon, this gives me a lot of food for thought!

THE SOLOMON PAPERS CLASS - OFFER

As we pursue this marvelous perception of reality, where free will is one of the most important principles of our existence, is that of the word "offer." Every aspect of this version of our reality is absolutely overflowing with "offers." Some are for our ultimate benefit, and some are not. It is up to us as individuals to do what we will with them with discernment.

For example, we are continually offered the opportunity to dwell as our best selves or let our ego take us into some very dark and harmful places. If we continue with those "questionable states of being," we become vulnerable to the dark thoughts and half-truths that we really want no part of.

If we fall into that trap, we could easily lose our spiritual compass. *Even then, there is still hope* because in this "reality," there is always hope and the chance to change. The "offer" to change and grow is always with us.

LIFE SAVER

Several years ago, I was fast asleep with my wife Valerie at my side. For some unknown reason, my breathing became quite irregular. She became aware of it and immediately reacted. She rolled me off the bed and pounded my chest, which restored my breathing to normal.

She literally saved my life.

To be clear, she's had my back ever since we met. I will forever be grateful for that experience with my "beloved partner for life." There have been many similar experiences in the following years.

THANK YOU, MY SWEET!

ACKNOWLEDGMENTS

To our Creator, who makes all of this possible. For without your love, none of this would exist. I stand in awe of the many gifts and blessings you offer to me each and every day.

To "The Solomon" who is the foundation of this entire work. For decades your wisdom and insight have been shared with countless students, clients, and friends. You have been largely responsible for my motivation to continue on my path and for shaping my outlook on my world, this planet, the universe, and beyond. You will always be a part of me and my quest for answers.

To Marva Mason for your tireless efforts in assisting with this work. You have spent countless hours editing and helping to get this book ready for publication. I couldn't have done this without you, Marva. Thank you for your loving support throughout the years we have known each other.

To Madison Land for your beautiful artwork for the book cover. Also, for your many years attending our Meditation Class in which "The Solomon" has been a significant factor. Your personal experience with "The Solomon" helped you to create a magnificent and artful representation of this work.

To Cynthia Stone, my profound appreciation for your guidance and expertise.

To my beautiful and artistic daughter, Lisa Baptiste. Thank you for your poignant contribution of the magical and dreamlike artwork that completes my vision for this combined effort. In my mind, you have always been well-qualified to contribute to any and all of my projects.

To my adored and eternal companion, Valerie A. Gudmundson. Thank you for the many hours of collaborative effort and never-ending faith in me and this work. It could not have been done without you and your love.

Last but certainly not least, I am grateful to my beloved meditation students, who have supported me throughout the years. No matter how many weeks, months or years you attended my class, you have left a permanent impression on me and my life. I have learned more from you than I have taught. I will love you all eternally.

ABOUT THE AUTHOR

Murry Grant Gudmundson was born in Salt Lake City but was mainly reared in Riverside, CA. He was baptized at the age of eight and graduated from Riverside Polytechnic High School. He has always lived a spiritual life, inspired by his parents' example.

As a young adult, he moved back to Utah, where he still lives. After attending the University of Utah for a short period of time, he received training in Alchemy from a private tutor, which gave him an introduction to the Metaphysical world. He has been a Presenter at several Past Life Regression Seminars which included references to his Alchemical training. Throughout the years, he has taught many Meditation, Past Life Regression, and Dreamwork classes. Grant's short publication on Dreamwork includes a recording of one of his Guided Meditations.

Grant and his wife Valerie enjoy a blended family of ten children. They currently reside in West Valley City, UT, with four cats. He learned to paint at age eighty and has continued to love this new hobby. They enjoy travels to the Caribbean and Mexico, as well as to the Oregon Coast.

A BOOK OF MESSAGES FROM SPIRIT

www.ingramcontent.com/pod-product-compliance
Lightning Source LLC
LaVergne TN
LVHW010030070426
835512LV00004B/53